GRASS CUTTER FARMING MASTERY

Raise And Profit From Your Own Grass Cutter Herd

An In-Depth Manual On Cuniculture For Beginners And Experienced Farmers Alike

Dr. Fabian Felicity

Table of Contents

CHAPTER ONE

Introduction

Grass cutter farming, sometimes known as cane rat farming, is becoming more popular as a profitable agricultural endeavor.

The demand for grass cutters, which are native to Africa but are now farmed all over the globe, is increasing owing to their tasty meat and minimal care needs.

This article will walk you through the necessary procedures to get started with grass-cutter farming, from understanding the animals to choosing the correct breed and establishing your grass-cutter farm.

Getting Started With Grasscutter Farming

Starting a grass-cutter farming business requires careful planning and a basic grasp of the demands of these distinct animals. Before getting into the technicalities of grasscutter farming, you need to assess your farm's purpose, market demand, and resource availability.

Grass cutters may be raised for meat production, breeding, or both, so selecting your main purpose will help you plan your strategy.

Research is an important part of getting started with grass-cutter farming. Learn about the traits, behaviors, and nutritional needs of lawn cutters. They are herbivores that eat grasses, leaves, and agricultural byproducts. Providing balanced and healthy food is critical for their health and productivity.

Understanding Grass Cutters

Grass cutters, also known as Thryonomys swinderianus, are rodents from the Thryonomyidae family. They are medium-sized creatures with stocky bodies, short legs, and a compact physique.

These rodents are notable for their robust and sharp incisors, which are designed for biting on tough plants.

In the wild, grass cutters are known to dig intricate tunnel networks for refuge and defense. Understanding their natural behavior is critical for providing appropriate dwelling circumstances on your grass cutter farm. Grass cutters are often more solitary than other livestock, and each breeding couple or individual should have its enclosure to reduce stress and territorial problems.

Choosing The Right Grass Cutter Breed

Choosing the proper kind of grass cutter is an important choice that may have a big influence on the success of your agricultural enterprise. There are various grass cutter breeds, each with its distinct qualities. The West African grass cutter, for example, is one of the most widely farmed varieties owing to its flexibility and relatively rapid development.

Consider your region's environment, the aim of your agricultural endeavor, and the availability of certain breeds. Some breeds are better suited for meat production, while others may be more prolific breeders, helping to ensure your farm's sustainability. In addition, consider the health and genetic heritage of the grass cutters you want to buy to guarantee a robust and disease-resistant breeding stock.

CHAPTER TWO

Setting Up Your Grass Cutter Farm

Providing an appropriate atmosphere for your lawn cutters is critical to their well-being and productivity. Begin by creating well-designed cages that resemble their natural environment. These enclosures should include shelters, food spaces, and plenty of room for the lawn cutters to walk about in.

Creating adequate burrows inside the enclosures is critical since grass cutters build tunnels for shelter and reproduction. Provide a variety of grasses and appropriate food products to maintain a well-balanced diet.

To keep your grass cutter herd healthy, schedule regular veterinarian check-ups and vaccines.

In addition to the physical layout, consider adopting a good management system for your grass cutter farm. Maintain precise records of breeding cycles, health indicators, and any treatments used. This information will be very useful for making educated choices and swiftly resolving possible difficulties.

To optimize the economic potential of your grass cutter farm, investigate marketing techniques and distribution channels for your goods.

Connect with local markets, restaurants, and people who are interested in unusual meats. Creating a brand for your lawn cutter items may also help them gain market appeal.

Grass-cutter farming offers a unique and intriguing option for agribusiness enthusiasts. Understanding the fundamentals of grasscutter farming, from biology and behavior to breed selection and farm structure, can help you launch a profitable and sustainable company.

Whether you want to raise meat, breed animals, or do both, careful planning, study, and devotion are critical to the long-term sustainability of your grass-cutter farm. With the proper expertise and dedication, you can convert your grass-cutter farming business into a satisfying and successful undertaking.

Creating The Ideal Habitat

The success of grasscutter farming is heavily dependent on the establishment of an optimum environment for these rodents. Grass cutters, also known as cane rats, are native to Sub-Saharan Africa and flourish in surroundings similar to their natural habitats.

When creating a habitat, it is critical to consider temperature, humidity, and shelter. These mice are very sensitive to changes in their surroundings, so providing a setting that closely replicates their natural environment would benefit their general well-being.

The habitat should feature a safe enclosure with enough room for the grass cutters to wander around and feed freely. native flora, such as grass and bushes, should be used to mimic the mice's native food and environment. To provide a healthy environment for the grass cutters, a balanced ecology inside the enclosure must be established.

Feeding And Nutrition Of Grass Cutters

Proper food and nutrition are critical to the effective raising of grass cutters. These rodents are herbivores, eating largely grasses, leaves, and plant stems. Mimicking their natural diet is critical for preserving their health and promoting healthy development. A well-balanced diet that includes a range of fresh, high-quality forage will supply the nutrients grass cutters need to flourish.

Supplementary feeding may be necessary to satisfy specific nutritional demands, particularly in areas where natural fodder is limited during certain seasons. Pelleted feeds with a balanced combination of vitamins and minerals may be used to enhance their diet. Monitoring the grass cutters' physical condition and changing their food properly is critical for preventing malnutrition or obesity.

Access to clean, fresh water is equally crucial. Grass cutters need constant availability of water to sustain their physiological activities and help in digesting. Regular monitoring of their water consumption is required to detect any health problems early.

Healthcare & Disease Prevention

Maintaining the health of grasscutters is essential for a

successful agricultural operation. Routine healthcare procedures and illness prevention strategies are critical to keeping the herd healthy. Regular health checks, performed by skilled veterinarians or experienced farm people, aid in the early detection of sickness and the prevention of disease transmission within the herd.

Vaccination programs suited to the individual requirements of lawn cutters should be created to protect workers from prevalent illnesses. Furthermore, quarantine protocols for new arrivals should be implemented to prevent infections from entering the herd. Strict biosecurity measures, such as adequate sanitation and hygiene practices, are required to reduce the danger of disease transmission.

Adequate shelter and ventilation in the habitat help to avoid sickness by lowering stress levels and fostering a healthy living environment. Addressing any indicators of sickness early, such as changes in behavior or appetite, is critical to preventing disease transmission and maintaining the grass cutters' general health.

CHAPTER THREE

Breeding And Reproduction Techniques

To maintain a consistent and healthy population, successful grass-cutter farming requires good breeding and reproductive processes. Understanding the reproductive biology of grasscutters is critical for improving breeding efforts.

These rodents have a short gestation time, and females may have numerous litters each year, making them prolific breeders.

Selective breeding for desired qualities including size, weight increase, and reproductive performance may assist enhance the herd's overall quality. Maintaining appropriate male-to-female ratios is critical for preventing violence and creating a pleasant breeding environment. Providing nesting boxes or quiet locations within the ecosystem encourages females to nest during their reproductive season.

Monitoring reproductive health is critical for identifying abnormalities that may impair fertility or effective child-raising. Introducing breeding pairs at the appropriate age and providing enough nourishment throughout the reproductive period help to ensure the breeding program's overall success.

Managing Grass Cutter Herd Dynamics

Grass-cutter herd dynamics are critical to the overall success of an agricultural enterprise. Understanding the social structure and behavior of these rodents is critical for successful herd management. Grass cutters are gregarious animals, and a healthy social structure among the herd is critical to their well-being.

Proper grouping of lawn cutters based on age, size, and compatibility helps to avoid aggressiveness and territorial problems. Overcrowding in the environment should be minimized to reduce stress and ensure that each individual has enough resources. Enrichments, like as hiding locations and climbing structures, provide mental activity and prevent boredom among the herd.

Regular monitoring of herd dynamics enables early intervention in the event of disputes or health concerns. It is critical to be alert for indicators of stress, aggressiveness, or injury and respond quickly. A well-managed and contented herd not only assures the welfare of the grass cutters but also helps to the overall success and sustainability of the agricultural operation.

To summarize, successful grass-cutter farming requires developing the right environment, concentrating on feeding and nutrition, adopting healthcare and disease prevention measures, utilizing effective breeding and reproduction procedures, and controlling grass-cutter herd dynamics. Farmers may create a healthy environment for grasscutters by emphasizing these factors, resulting in a long-term and profitable business.

Harvesting And Processing Grass Cutters

Grass cutter farming, also known as cane rat farming, is gaining popularity as a profitable agricultural endeavor. One important feature of this endeavor is the effective collecting and processing of grass cutters. Harvesting success necessitates the use of appropriate procedures and instruments.

To begin, determining the optimal time for harvesting is critical. Grass cutters are typically ready for harvesting when they reach a certain weight and size, which is generally between 1.5 and 2 kg.

This guarantees that the meat's quality is excellent. Harvesting may be done humanely to reduce stress on the animals and provide greater meat quality. Specially constructed cages and handling equipment may help make harvesting more efficient and humane.

The processing step begins once the harvest has been completed. This includes dressing and preparing meat for the market. Clean and sanitary processing facilities are critical to ensuring the quality and safety of grass cutter products. Proper sanitation methods throughout processing limit the danger of contamination and guarantee that the finished goods fulfill health requirements.

Furthermore, investing in proper processing equipment, such as meat grinders and vacuum sealers, improves efficiency and increases product shelf life. Another important consideration is packing; vacuum-sealed packaging not only retains the freshness of the meat but also makes the items more appealing to consumers. Efficient harvesting and processing are critical to the success of any grass-cutter farming operation.

Marketing And Selling Grass Cutter Products

After successfully harvesting and processing grass cutters, the next critical step is to market and sell the products. A strong marketing strategy is required to reach potential customers and generate demand for grass cutter products.

Understanding the target market is essential. Identifying consumer preferences, demographics, and purchasing behavior helps to tailor the marketing strategy. Grass-cutter meat is frequently marketed as a lean and healthy option, so emphasizing its nutritional value can be a persuasive strategy.

Building an online presence is also crucial in today's digital age. Creating a website or using social media platforms enables farmers to promote their goods and interact with prospective buyers. Customers may easily make purchases and learn more about the farm and its methods via online channels.

Collaboration with local grocery shops, restaurants, and farmers' markets may broaden the reach of grass-cutter goods. Offering samples to prospective consumers in these areas may raise awareness and interest. Positive word-of-mouth may be an effective way to establish a reputation for high-quality lawn cutter items.

Moreover, branding has an important role. Creating a unique and memorable brand identity distinguishes lawn cutter goods from the competition. This involves developing a memorable logo, producing eye-catching packaging, and building a consistent brand messaging.

CHAPTER FOUR
Financial Plan For Grass Cutter Farming

Budgeting, cost estimates, income forecasting, and risk management are all part of grass-cutter farming's financial planning. Creating a detailed financial strategy is critical for the long-term viability and profitability of the agricultural business.

Begin by evaluating the initial expenditure necessary to start up the grass cutter farm. This covers the expenditures of collecting breeding couples, erecting cages, procuring feed, and establishing processing facilities. It is critical to do extensive market research to identify the potential demand for lawn cutter items in the target region.

Budgeting for ongoing expenditures like feed, veterinary care, and utilities is critical for day-to-day operations. Keeping an eye on these expenditures allows farmers to make better choices and find areas where spending may be reduced.

Revenue prediction is predicting the money produced by the sale of lawn cutter items. This necessitates an accurate estimate of the projected yield, pricing strategy, and market demand. Establishing a competitive but profitable pricing structure is critical to financial sustainability.

Risk management is another important aspect of financial planning. Disease outbreaks, market changes, and unexpected weather conditions all influence the grass cutter farm's performance. Diversifying revenue sources, investing in insurance, and adopting biosecurity measures may all assist in reducing these risks.

Challenges And Solutions For Grass Cutter Farming

While grass-cutter farming is a profitable enterprise, it is not without its problems. Identifying and tackling these difficulties is critical to the enterprise's long-term success.

One recurrent difficulty is a lack of understanding and acceptability of grass-fed beef in particular markets. Overcoming this barrier necessitates educational programs that enlighten customers about the nutritional advantages and ethical procedures involved with grass-cutter farming.

Disease management is another key difficulty. Grass cutters are vulnerable to a variety of illnesses, and an epidemic may decimate a field. Strict biosecurity controls, frequent health checks, and close collaboration with veterinary specialists are critical for disease prevention and management.

Market rivalry and price constraints may also provide difficulties for grass-cutter producers. To combat this, diversifying goods, researching specialized markets, and building a strong brand presence may help the farm stand out from the competition.

Climate and environmental conditions may influence feed availability and quality, impacting grasscutters' general health and productivity. Creating contingency planning for unfavorable weather situations and researching sustainable agricultural techniques may help boost resilience.

Conclusion

Finally, grass-cutter farming offers a great opportunity for agribusiness enterprises. Efficient harvesting and processing, intelligent marketing, and good financial planning are critical components to success. Despite the hurdles, with competent management and a proactive attitude to issue resolution, grass cutter farming may be a long-term and gratifying venture. As the need for alternative and lean meat sources grows, the grass cutter business is poised for expansion and profitability.